LIBRARY

John Malam

CONTENTS

The fold-out section at the start of this book shows the library building from the outside. Open it up to reveal a cutaway view of the inside, with a key to what happens in each room. After this you will find a plan of the lending library.

Belitha Press

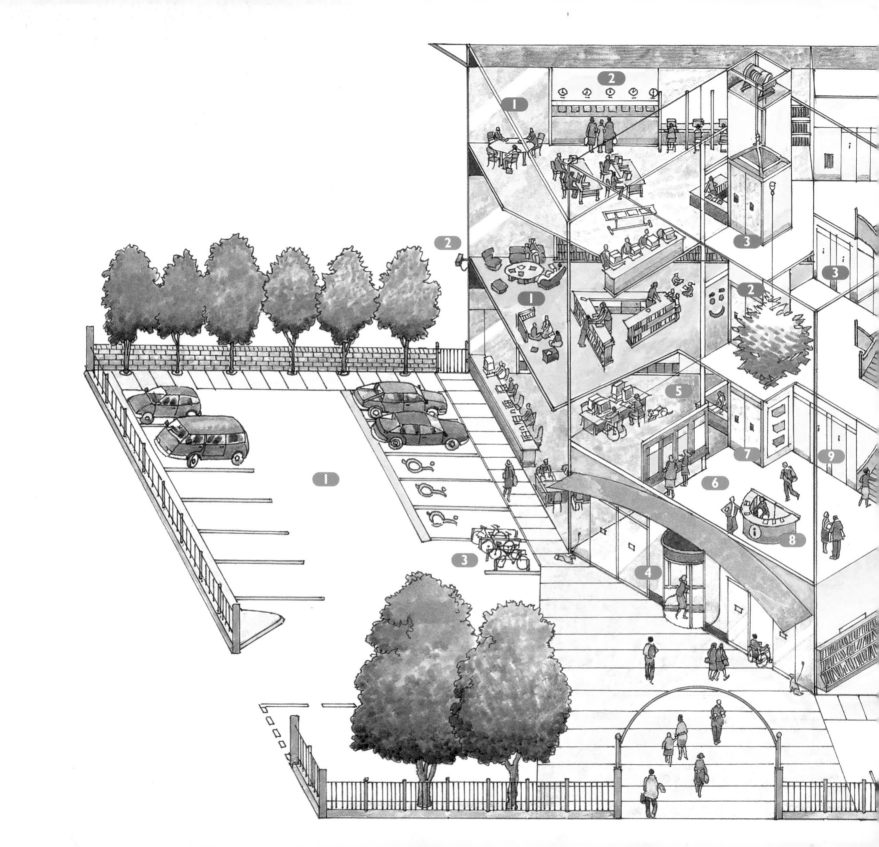

nside a library

his picture shows the inside of a large public library. The building is imaginary, but it gives a good idea of what happens in a real library. floors are colour-coded and the rooms are bered. To find out what happens in each room, the key on either side of the main picture.

ground floor of the library is represented by , the first floor by blue and the second floor by en. As you read the book, you will find the colours ated along the edge of the pages, to show which r you are on. To find the department you are reading ut, use the ⊜ symbol at the top of each page. It is a lified plan of the three floors. On each right-hand page will also find a list of the department's room numbers.

ne of the more unusual words used in this book explained in the glossary on page 30.

 # Ground floor

1 Car park
Visitors park here free of charge. There are several spaces for disabled drivers.

2 Security cameras
Two cameras operate 24 hours a day – in the car park and at the rear of the building.

3 Bicycle rack

4 Main entrance
Wide electric doors without steps make it easy for everyone to enter the building.

5 Special needs library
This department is for users with special needs, such as the partially-sighted or blind. It contains Braille books and machines that magnify text or read books aloud.

6 Exhibition area
In this area, the library displays paintings, photographs or crafts made by local artists and children.

7 Lifts

8 Information desk
Staff here answer visitors' questions and direct people to different parts of the library.

9 Toilets

10 Meeting room
This room is used for workshops, exhibitions and author readings.

11 Staff car park

12 Lending library
This is the largest room in the building, containing books on every subject. All the books can be taken out by users.

13 Issue desk
Books are borrowed and returned here. Electronic security barriers prevent thefts.

14 Newspaper area
The library has a large stock of newspapers and magazines which can only be read in the building.

15 Book stacks
Old or rarely-used books are kept on these movable shelves. They can be borrowed by special request.

16 Mobile library unit
This vehicle tours the surrounding area, bringing a selection of books to people who cannot visit the library.

17 Delivery bay
New books are delivered here, at the rear of the building.

What is a library?

A library is a building where recorded information is kept, in any form – as books, maps, newspapers, magazines, microfilms, tapes, CD-ROMs and photographs. But a library is much more than just the building – the collection itself is called a library too.

The largest libraries have millions of items in their collections. These range from 5000-year-old poems written on clay tablets to today's best-selling novels. Library collections are looked after by skilled librarians, archivists, conservators, bookbinders and information technologists.

There are many types of library, each designed to be used by a particular group of people. The most common type is the public library. Most towns have one or more public libraries. They are open to everyone free of charge, for entertainment, pleasure, education and business.

There are all sorts of specialist libraries too. These include university libraries, medical libraries, legal libraries and architecture libraries.

This book looks at how a modern public library works. It is the type of large library found in a major city such as London or New York. Many small public libraries do not have as many departments – perhaps just a lending library and a reference section.

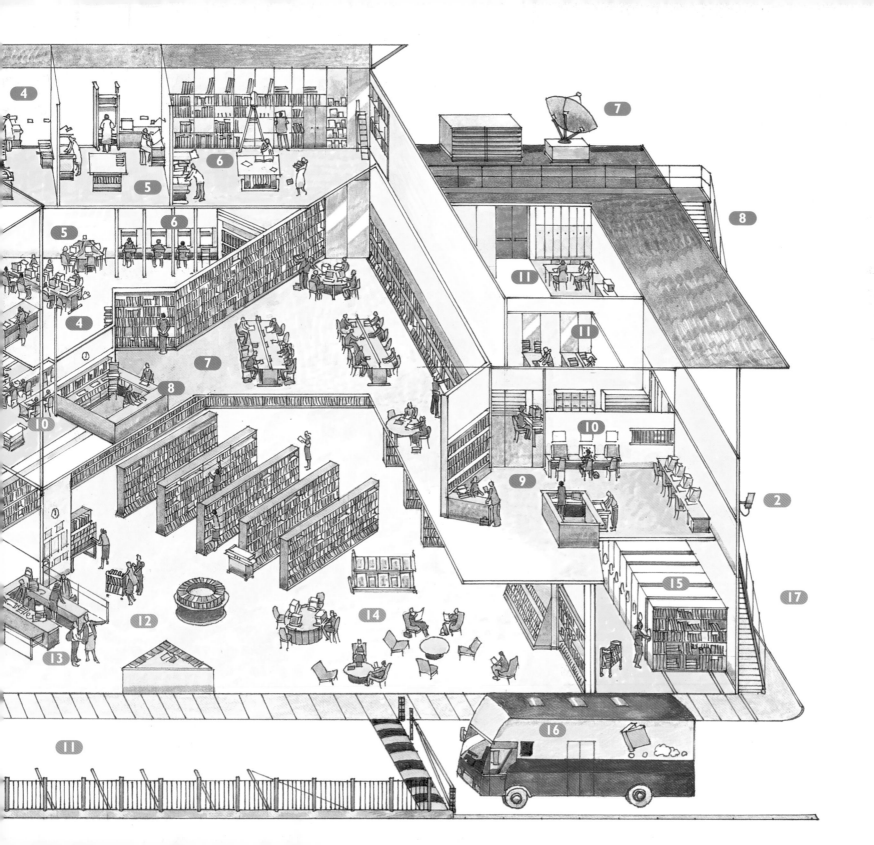

First floor

1 Children's library
Young users have access to books, magazines, toys and computers in this part of the library.

2 Lifts

3 Toilets

4 Audiovisual and multimedia library
Library users can borrow CDs, videos and cassettes from this department. They also use the Internet and CD-ROMs.

5 Internet cluster
These computers are permanently linked to the Internet. Users often have to book in advance, and usually pay per hour.

6 Listening booths
In these booths library users listen to tapes and audio CDs through headphones, and have a desk to make notes at.

7 Reference library
The books here cannot be borrowed – they have to be read in the library. They include atlases, encyclopaedias and dictionaries. There are lots of desks for users to work at.

8 Reference enquiry desk
The reference library has a large number of books and journals in storage. Users can ask for them at the enquiry desk.

9 Local studies library
This department contains books, photographs, maps and pamphlets about the local area. Only some of them can be borrowed.

10 Microfilm readers
To save space, the library's stock of old newspapers is copied on to microfilm and viewed with these special readers.

11 Staff room and offices
Here library staff carry out all the administration that keeps the library running smoothly.

Second floor

1 Business library
This department contains the latest information on company share prices, as well as lists of businesses and the services they provide.

2 Teletext monitors
News headlines and financial updates are displayed on this bank of teletext screens.

3 Lifts

4 Bindery
In this room, old or fragile books are given new, strong covers to protect them. Sets of newspapers and magazines are bound into single volumes too.

5 Conservation
Valuable and fragile books are repaired here by conservators.

6 Rare books
This department contains items that may be hundreds or even thousands of years old. Users have to make an appointment to visit the department.

7 Satellite dish
This dish allows the library to pick up hundreds of satellite TV channels. The programmes are shown in the children's, business and multimedia departments.

8 Fire escape

In a typical lending library, fiction titles are arranged according to the surname of the author, from A to Z. Non-fiction books are grouped by subject, according to the Dewey Decimal System (see page 14). There is a large selection of the latest newspapers and magazines, as well as old books for sale.

FICTION A – P

FICTION Q – Z

Foreign language fiction

Large print fiction

Community information

001–100 General topics

100–200 Philosophy & psychology

200–300 Religion
300–400 Social sciences

400–500 Languages

500–600 Science & mathematics

600–700 Technology
700–800 The arts

800–900 Literature

900–999 Geography & history

NEWSPAPERS & MAGAZINES

IN

Issue desk

OUT

Books for sale

Oversize books

Magazines

Seating area

Information

Lending library

The busiest part of the building is the lending library – a large, open-plan room filled with books, magazines and newspapers. Most items in here are for adults. Children have their own library.

The lending library is open from early morning until the evening, so people can visit after work. All the items can be borrowed for a short time. This is usually between one and four weeks.

There are thousands of different books in the lending library. Catalogues help people find what they want quickly and easily. An important part of a librarian's work is to keep the catalogue up-to-date and accurate.

Most libraries keep their catalogue on computer, but a few still use printed cards kept inside drawers. A computer catalogue is faster and easier to use.

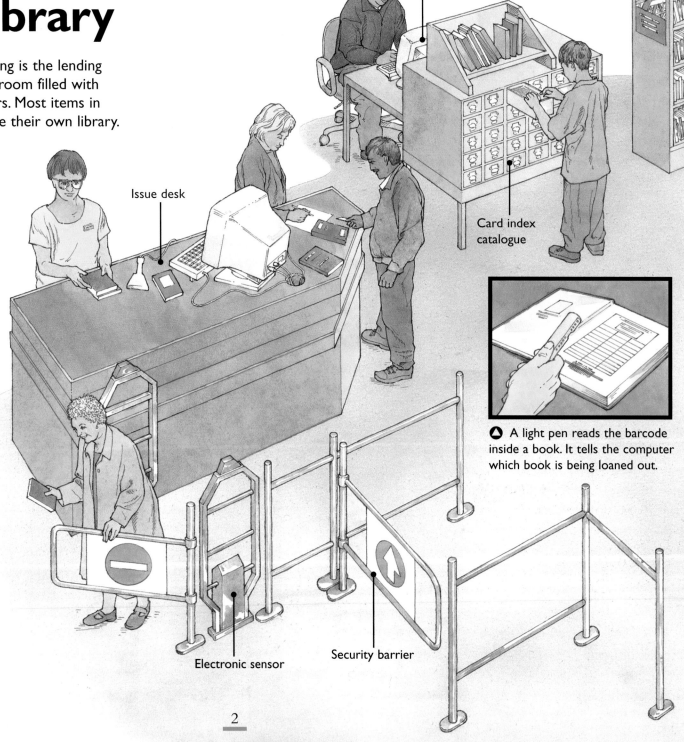

Computer catalogue

Issue desk

Card index catalogue

▲ A light pen reads the barcode inside a book. It tells the computer which book is being loaned out.

Electronic sensor

Security barrier

12
13
14

⬥ The computerized catalogue shows whether books are in stock or out on loan, how many copies there are in the collection, and whether any other libraries in the area have copies.

Photocopier

The catalogue is divided into two sections. The author index lists each item by the surname of its author, from A to Z. The subject index groups books according to what they are about, also in alphabetical order. To find out what books there are on any topic, from America to zoos, the subject catalogue is the place to look.

There is a metal ribbon, called a trigger strip, inside every book. This is magnetized when the book is in the library. Before a book is loaned out, the strip is demagnetized by passing it over a desensitizer. This stops an electronic sensor from triggering the alarm at the exit. The book is then stamped with the date it is due back at the library.

The computer keeps track of every book in the collection. The librarian can look up a user's details to find out how many books they have borrowed and when they are due back.

Special needs library

One of the rooms in the library is for people who have special needs. For example, some library users cannot see well enough to read by themselves. Here they use machines which act as their eyes.

A Kurzweil reader is a machine that converts printed words into speech, just as if someone was reading a book out loud. The speed is controlled by the listener – on average, it reads about 200 words a minute. It even speaks in different accents. The user can make a tape recording to take home and play back whenever they want.

▲ A Kurzweil reader scans a page from a book, then reads it through headphones so that other users are not disturbed.

Kurzweil reader

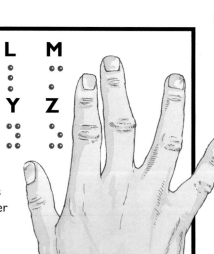

A	B	C	D	E	F	G	H	I	J	K	L	M

N	O	P	Q	R	S	T	U	V	W	X	Y	Z

▲ Braille is named after its inventor, Louis Braille, who devised a system of reading raised dots in 1829. Braille is written on a machine called a brailler, a kind of typewriter with only six keys.

▶ People read Braille by moving their fingertips across lines of raised dots. Each letter of the alphabet has its own pattern of dots. Numbers can be written in Braille too.

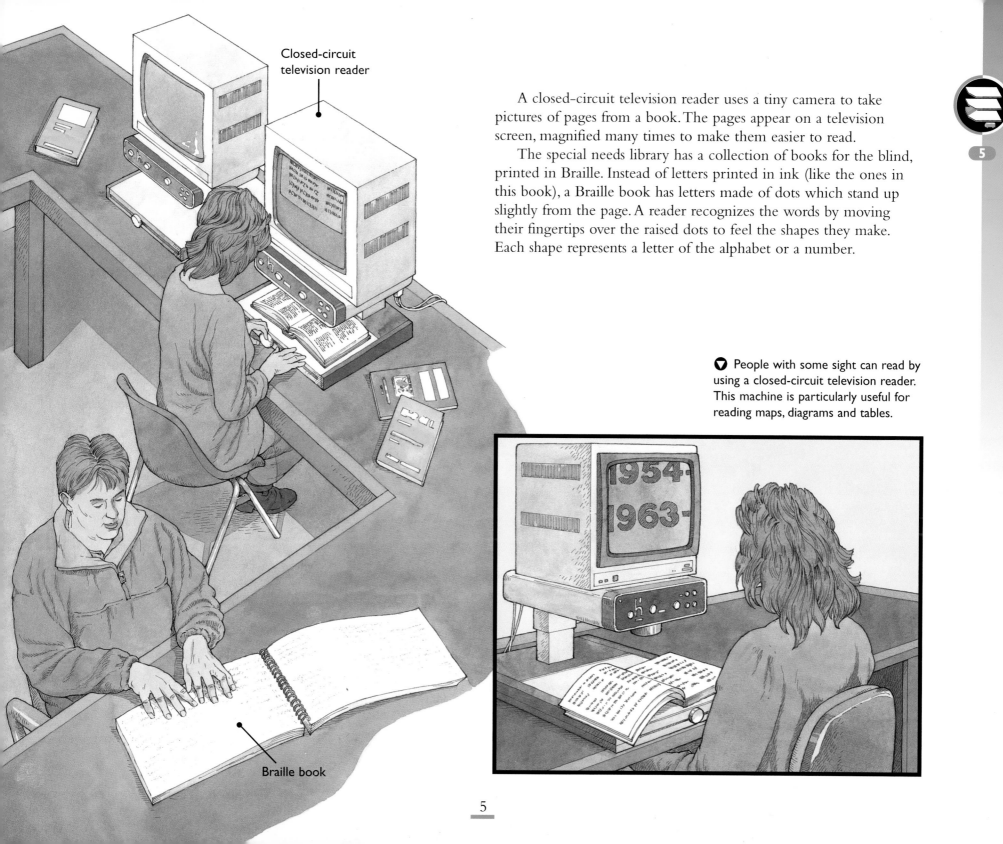

Closed-circuit television reader

Braille book

A closed-circuit television reader uses a tiny camera to take pictures of pages from a book. The pages appear on a television screen, magnified many times to make them easier to read.

The special needs library has a collection of books for the blind, printed in Braille. Instead of letters printed in ink (like the ones in this book), a Braille book has letters made of dots which stand up slightly from the page. A reader recognizes the words by moving their fingertips over the raised dots to feel the shapes they make. Each shape represents a letter of the alphabet or a number.

▼ People with some sight can read by using a closed-circuit television reader. This machine is particularly useful for reading maps, diagrams and tables.

Mobile library

Not everyone can travel to the library – so the library goes to them. The mobile library service takes books to people who may live many kilometres away, or who may be too ill to leave their homes.

Each mobile library vehicle carries about 3000 items. These are mostly books, but there are also videos, cassettes and CD-ROMs. Specially-made shelves hold everything safely in place.

The mobile library visits many different places in the local community throughout the week. It visits five or six places each day, and stays for about an hour each time. It stops at homes for the elderly, isolated villages, and even prisons. Some vehicles are fitted with lifts. They are used by the elderly and by people with disabilities who may not be able to climb up the steps of the vehicle.

Some mobile libraries visit schools as part of the library's education service. They are stocked with books to help children with schoolwork, as well as with popular story books by favourite authors.

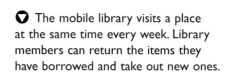

▼ The mobile library visits a place at the same time every week. Library members can return the items they have borrowed and take out new ones.

▲ Volunteers help to run the books on wheels service for people who cannot get to the library.

Visually-impaired people use the library's postal service. Borrowers tell the library which books they would like to hear on tape, and the cassettes are posted to them. In Britain, this service is free, because the Post Office does not charge for the postage.

The books on wheels service is for people who cannot visit the main library or the mobile library. Volunteers put together a selection of books, CDs, cassettes and even jigsaws. Every few weeks they visit people in their own homes or in hospital.

Children's library

Children have their own library, where they can borrow books, videos, audio tapes and CDs.

The children's library looks very different from the main lending library. The shelves are lower and there are book boxes on the floor, filled with picture books for young children and books for babies. Some shelves look like boats, trains or characters from children's stories. There are lots of toys for the youngest children to play with.

The books are grouped according to their subject. For example, information books about ballet are grouped together, as are all the fact books about space, horses, dinosaurs and so on. Story books are usually shelved in alphabetical order, according to the surnames of the authors.

◀ The children's library has lots of novelty books, with pop-up pictures, flaps and wheels. Television and film tie-ins are popular too.

Listening post

Low shelves

◀ Every book has a catalogue code. The number 910 means these books are about pirates. The letter J shows they are junior books. The letter I stands for information books. The codes can vary from one library to another.

Book box

Young children usually visit the library with a parent or teacher to choose books they want to borrow. They may come to listen to stories read by a librarian, a teacher or an author. Older children come on their own, looking for books to read for pleasure, or for information books to help with schoolwork.

There is a small collection of books from around the world, printed in languages such as Chinese, Hindustani, Arabic and French. They are for children who can read and speak other languages.

The library also has a collection of information books, such as encyclopaedias, on CD-ROM and DVD (digital versatile disc). These combine words, pictures, sound and video clips on computer.

CD-ROM and DVD computer

▶ A librarian uses a video camera linked to a computer to read a story book to a group of schoolchildren in another town.

Audiovisual and multimedia library

Today's libraries keep up to date with the latest technology. Users are as likely to use a computer to find information as they are to look it up in a book.

The audiovisual and multimedia library is stocked with music cassettes, compact discs (CDs), language courses, books on tape, computer software, CD–ROMs, DVDs, videos and pictures. Everything is listed in the library catalogue, in much the same way as books.

Users can borrow the latest music releases on tape or CD. Listening booths allow people to listen to the music before deciding whether or not to borrow the recording.

◀ One CD-ROM can store as many words as a whole shelf of books, complete with hundreds of pictures and sounds.

Internet, CD-ROM and computer area

Listening booth

Audio books are novels recorded on to tape. The stories are often read by well-known actors. A book may have to be shortened, or abridged, to fit on to one cassette. The plot of the story stays the same. Audio books can be taken out on loan, or listened to inside the library through headphones.

Many libraries have computers linked to the Internet. A user has access to libraries all over the world, searching for information which their own library may not have. A large library may even have its own site on the World Wide Web, with information about its collections.

Other computers are for information CD-ROMs. An Internet link may allow a user to go directly from a CD-ROM encyclopaedia to related websites, to find even more information about a subject. Pages can be downloaded and printed out on a library printer.

⬥ Before a video can be taken from the library, the security tag is removed by this machine. If the tag is not taken off, it sets off an alarm as the video passes through the security barrier at the exit.

Cassette player

Cassette tapes

Special events

Many libraries are also community centres which hold exhibitions, author readings, plays and evening classes.

Part of the library foyer is set aside as an exhibition space. The work of local artists and photographers is displayed on its walls, while cases display handmade craft objects. The exhibition items are usually on sale to the public.

Sometimes the library is turned into a theatre, where actors perform short plays, usually for children. These events often take place during the school holidays, and are designed to encourage children to use the library as much as possible.

Authors and illustrators visit the library to talk about their books. An author might read a few pages, while an illustrator may talk about drawing the pictures. At the end of the event, they answer questions from the audience and sign copies of the books.

△ Local artists display paintings in the library's exhibition area. Their pictures often show scenes of well-known places in the area.

◁ Libraries organize craft activities for children during school holidays. These include painting and pottery.

▶ Visiting theatre groups use the children's library to stage short plays or drama workshops. Children are sometimes given parts to perform.

Adult craft activities are usually held in the early evening. People can learn how to make and do a wide range of different things. These include painting or stencilling on to pottery, flower arranging and genealogy (researching family trees). Children's activities are held after school or during the holidays.

Local clubs and societies often hold their meetings in the library. These include photographic societies, writers' workshops, stamp clubs, local history groups and many more.

Reference library

Reference books include encyclopaedias, dictionaries and atlases. Many of them are expensive to buy, some are very big, and some are in sets made up of several parts. Books in the reference library cannot be borrowed.

The reference library is the place to find old copies of newspapers or magazines. Some are stored on shelves, but nowadays many are copied on to microfilm, microfiche or CD. Copying them saves space and prevents the originals being damaged. One microfilm stores about 20 large newspapers, while a CD can hold hundreds.

The reference library is a place of information and learning. Because it is quiet, students come here to study for exams. None of the books can be taken from the library, so there are lots of tables and seats for people to work at.

If a user asks for a book which the reference library doesn't have, it can be ordered on loan from another library. This could be anywhere in the world. The book usually arrives after a few days. The user reads it in the reference department before it is returned to its own library.

◀ An encyclopaedia made up of eight separate books, or volumes. There are far too many pages to put into one book.

Photocopier

Melvil Dewey (1851–1931) was an American librarian who invented a system of classifying books in 1876. The Dewey Decimal System of Classification is still used by libraries all over the world. It is a decimal system because it has ten basic divisions, into which every book can be fitted.	**The ten basic divisions of the Dewey Decimal System**	
	000	General topics
	100	Philosophy and psychology
	200	Religion
	300	Social sciences
	400	Language
	500	Natural sciences and mathematics
	600	Technology
	700	The arts
	800	Literature
	900	Geography and history

Reference books cannot be taken from the library

Microfilm is similar to camera film. Pages from books, newspapers and magazines are photographed on to the film. A microfilm reader enlarges the tiny images, which are projected on to a screen.

7

8

Word processor

Information desk

Local studies library

The local studies library is a collection of items about the local area, some of which are hundreds of years old. It can be a very busy place – so busy that users have to make appointments to come here.

The local studies library contains:
- books, pamphlets, newspapers and magazines about the area;
- parish registers recording births, marriages and deaths;
- photographs of people and buildings;
- directories of streets and the people who lived in them;
- maps, prints and drawings, many showing how the area looked before the first photographs were taken in the 1840s;
- letters and diaries written by people from the area;
- business documents from local companies;
- ephemera (everyday items such as posters, catalogues, price lists and railway timetables, which tell a story about the area's past).

Unlike the other parts of the library, most of the collection is kept out of sight of the public. A user fills in a request form, giving details of the item they want to see. Most items cannot be borrowed from the local studies library – they have to be used in the department.

Some people use the library to trace their family tree. They start by checking parish records and census information. Others might be interested in people or companies from the area. Authors writing books about the region come here to carry out research and look for pictures.

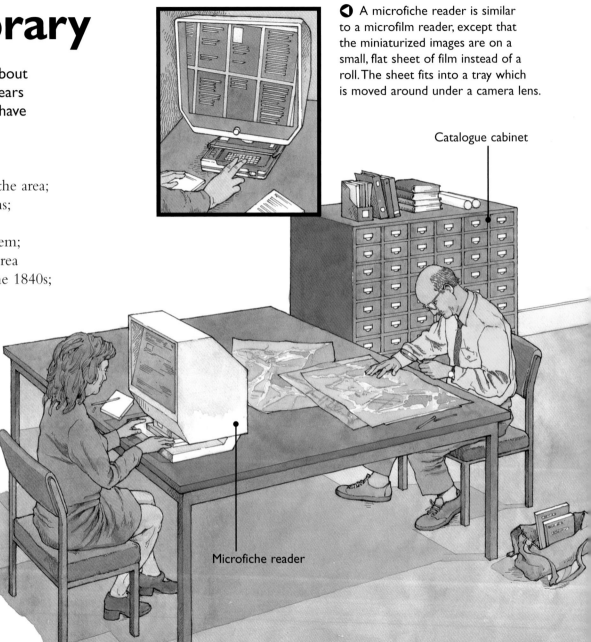

◀ A microfiche reader is similar to a microfilm reader, except that the miniaturized images are on a small, flat sheet of film instead of a roll. The sheet fits into a tray which is moved around under a camera lens.

Catalogue cabinet

Microfiche reader

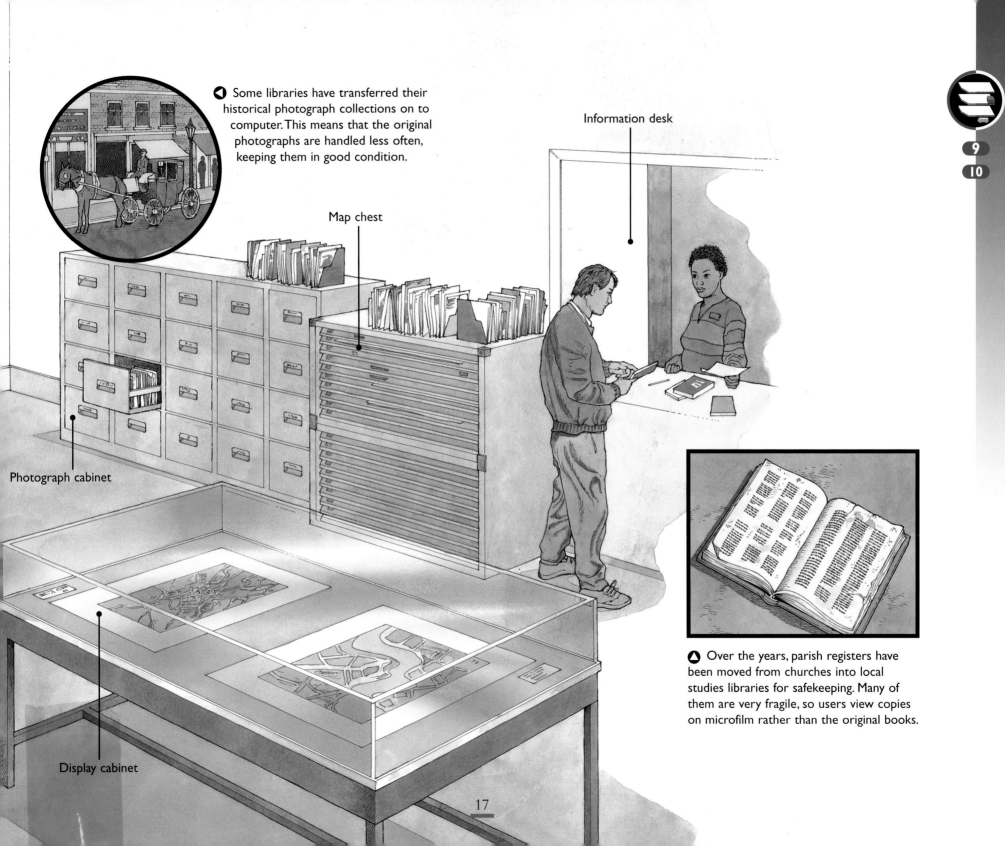

Some libraries have transferred their historical photograph collections on to computer. This means that the original photographs are handled less often, keeping them in good condition.

Information desk

Map chest

Photograph cabinet

Display cabinet

Over the years, parish registers have been moved from churches into local studies libraries for safekeeping. Many of them are very fragile, so users view copies on microfilm rather than the original books.

Business library

The business library is a very specialized department. Business people come here to find information about companies, the things they make, facts and figures about groups of people, and the laws of other countries.

Much of the information in the business library changes very quickly. To give users the latest information about companies, the department is linked to a network of computers. Business news is displayed on teletext monitors.

Other people come here to use international business directories. These list companies from all over the world, with information on their products and services, addresses and phone numbers.

The business library offers several ways for people to keep in touch with colleagues around the world. Computers are linked to the Internet, so users can send and collect e-mail messages. A videophone allows two people on opposite sides of the world to have a conversation and see each other on a computer screen at the same time.

◀ Information in the business library comes in many forms. Apart from books, there are spiral-bound reports, loose-leaf folders, videos, microfilms, CDs and cassettes.

Reference books and directories

Information desk

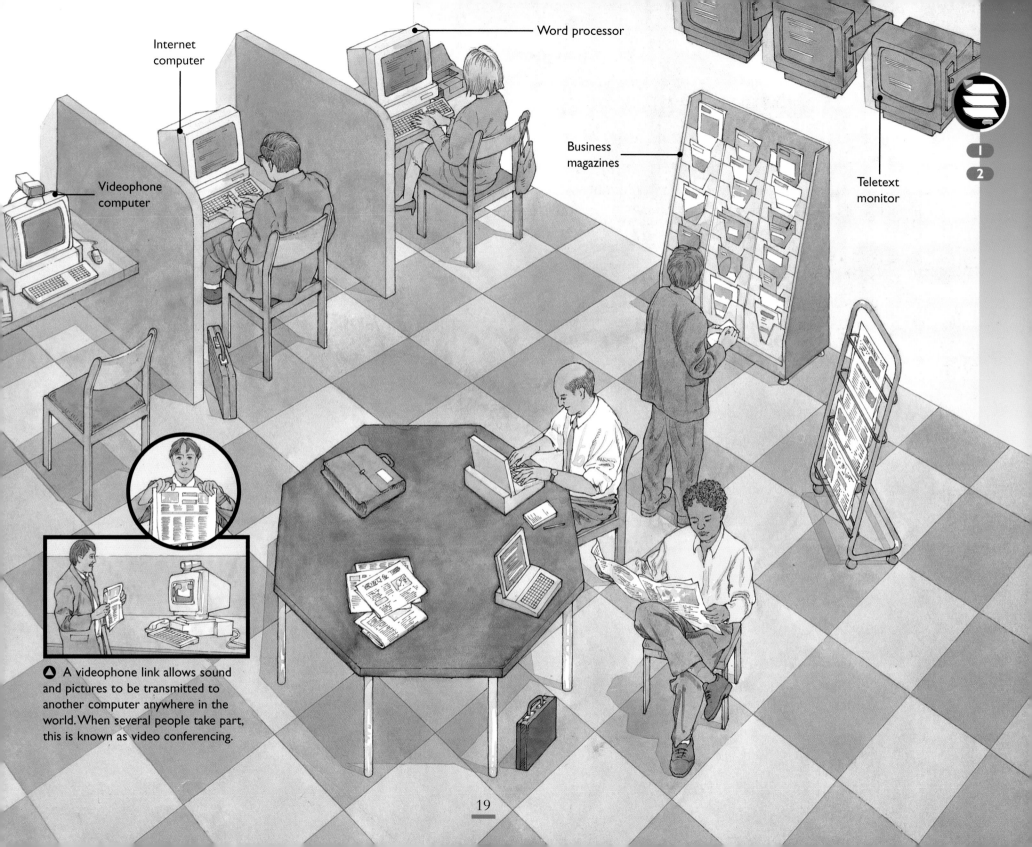

Internet
computer

Word processor

Videophone
computer

Business
magazines

Teletext
monitor

🔺 A videophone link allows sound
and pictures to be transmitted to
another computer anywhere in the
world. When several people take part,
this is known as video conferencing.

Rare book library

The rare book library is like a small museum – some of the items are thousands of years old. Light levels are kept low, because sunlight fades and discolours old books. The items in the collection are too valuable to be loaned out from the department.

Librarians wear cotton gloves when they handle rare books. The gloves prevent oils from their fingers marking the pages. Rare book display cases are made from materials which do not give off harmful gases. Oak, for instance, gives off a gas which can harm old paper.

Copying pages from rare books can also cause problems. The library has a special copier which does not squash books when they are copied. A book is placed face up beneath a camera, which is in the top of the machine. A photograph of the page is taken and printed out on an ordinary photocopier nearby.

The oldest items here are clay tablets with wedge-shaped signs pressed into them. These are from the Middle East, where writing was invented about 5000 years ago. Some other types of rare books are shown on page 21.

Glass-fronted bookcases protect rare books

Camera

Rare book photocopier

◀ A 3000-year-old clay tablet from the Middle East. The writing on it is called cuneiform, which means wedge-shaped. Prayers, spells, stories and lists of goods were all written in cuneiform.

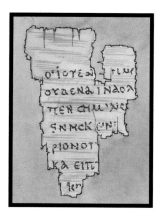

◀ A Bible fragment dating from around 200 AD. It is written in Greek on papyrus, an early type of paper made from water reed stems.

◀ A page from a 600-year-old book written by the Maya people of Central America. They wrote using oval signs called glyphs.

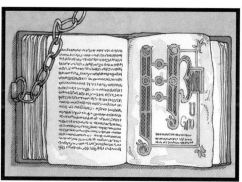

◀ In the Middle Ages, library books in European monasteries and cathedrals were chained to the shelves so no-one could steal them. They were written by hand on animal skin called vellum.

▶ A page from one of the earliest printed books, from the late 1400s. Books from this period are known as incunables. Librarians call them inkies for short.

Conservation

Documents written or printed on paper are fragile. An old book might have loose or torn pages, or its cover might have come off. This damage can be repaired. If a piece of a page is missing, it can be patched. Paper that is too brittle to handle can be strengthened. This is the work of the conservation department.

One of the greatest dangers old books and documents face (apart from fire), is damage from acid. Books and newspapers less than 100 years old are most at risk, because the paper they are made from comes from wood pulp. Natural acids in trees remain in the wood pulp when it is made into paper. Over many years the acid leaks through the paper, turning it brown and brittle. Paper more than 100 years old is often made from rags and plants. Acid damage is less of a problem with these types of paper.

To remove the acid from the pages of a book, it is carefully taken apart until all its pages are loose. Each page is soaked in special water. This washes away the acid and cleans the paper, but leaves it weak. To strengthen it, the paper is dried and then sprayed with a gelatine solution. This holds the paper fibres together, making the page strong enough to handle once again.

Tears and holes are repaired with a special tissue paper. This very thin, transparent material is pasted on to the page and lasts for many years.

When every page has been cleaned and repaired, the book goes to the bindery to be given a new cover.

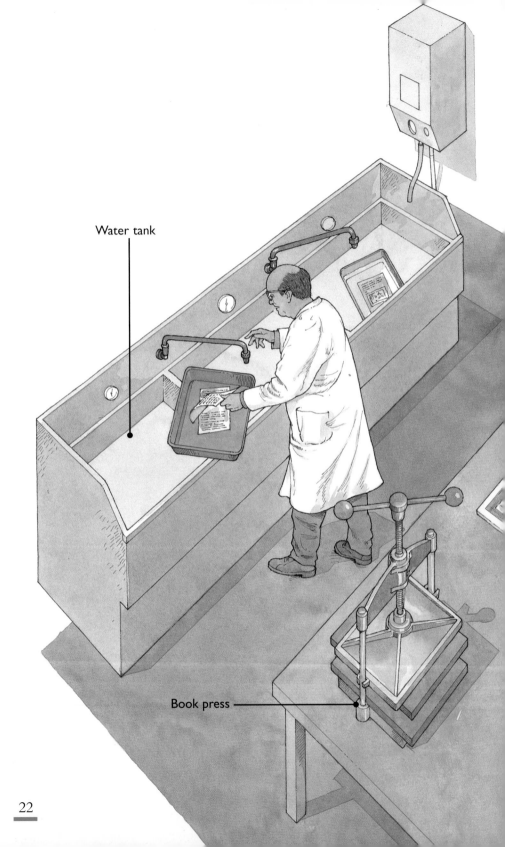

Water tank

Book press

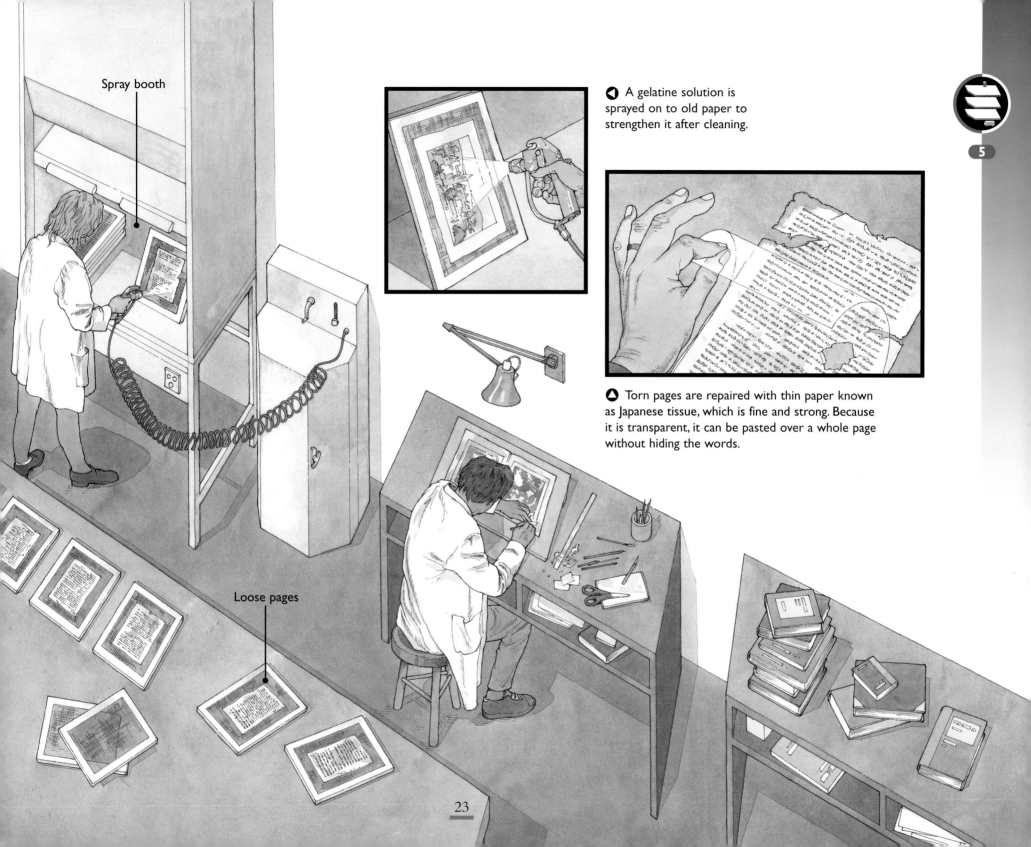

Spray booth

A gelatine solution is sprayed on to old paper to strengthen it after cleaning.

Torn pages are repaired with thin paper known as Japanese tissue, which is fine and strong. Because it is transparent, it can be pasted over a whole page without hiding the words.

Loose pages

Bindery

Books are given new covers in the bindery department. Sets of newspapers and magazines are bound together into single volumes. This makes them easier to store and use.

1 Before a book can have a new cover fitted, it has to be unbound. The old cover is taken off, and the glue and thread which hold the pages together are removed.

2 The loose pages are stacked together in the right order. The stack is called a book block.

3 The block of paper is put into a powerful guillotine machine. A blade trims each edge in a single cut.

4 Heavy sheets of paper, called endpapers, are glued to the first and last pages of the book block. The spine of the book block is given a rounded shape by tapping it with a hammer.

5 The rounded spine is strengthened with a thick layer of glue and a piece of cloth called gauze. The glue and the gauze hold the pages of the book block together. To make the book even stronger, sometimes the pages are sewn together at the spine.

6 If the book is to be a hardback, the pieces of board that make the cover stiff are cut to size with a guillotine.

7 The boards are covered with leather, cloth or a cheaper material to create the new cover.

8 The endpapers on the book block are glued to the inside of the cover.

9 A book press squeezes the book block and the cover together until the glue has dried.

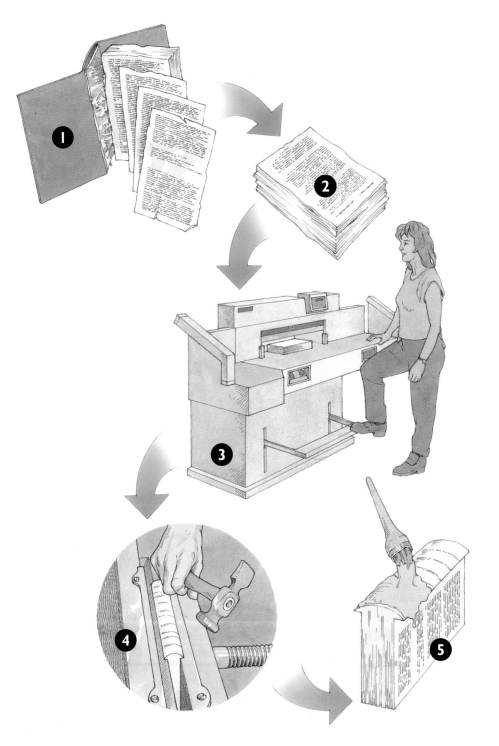

10 The leather cover of a valuable book is decorated with patterns stamped on it by hand. The title and author's name are also stamped on it, letter by letter, using a sheet of gold leaf.

11 Less valuable books or sets of magazines have their titles stamped on by machine, using coloured tape.

◀ This print wheel is fitted to a machine which stamps the title and author's name on to a book cover.

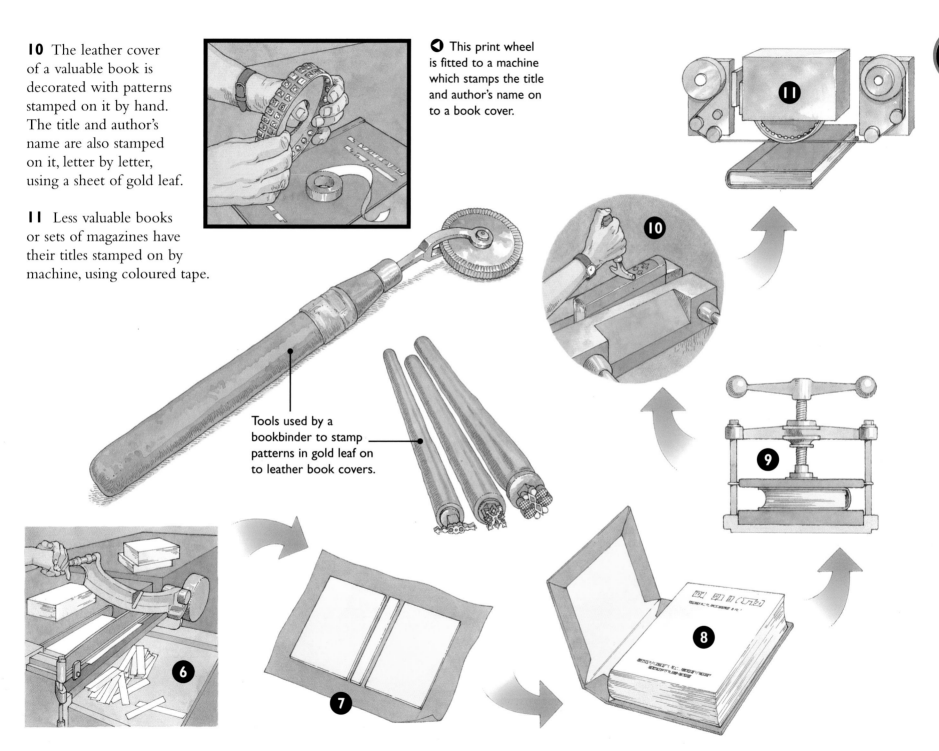

Tools used by a bookbinder to stamp patterns in gold leaf on to leather book covers.

25

Library history

Ashurbanipal, king of Assyria, establishes the world's first great library, at Nineveh (in present-day Iraq). The collection is made up of more than 20 000 clay tablets containing poems, spells and stories.

600s BC

Ptolemy I, pharaoh of Egypt, founds the most famous library of ancient times, at Alexandria. Over the next few centuries the collection grows to around 500 000 papyrus scrolls.

300s BC

Libraries are built in China during the Qin Dynasty (221–206 BC). One copy of every book in the empire is placed in the emperor's library. By 800 AD the library contains 5000 books.

200s BC

During the Dark Ages, monasteries are the main centres of learning and knowledge in Europe.

500s AD to 1000 AD

Europe's first national library is founded in Prague, the capital of the present-day Czech Republic.

1366

600 BC to 1747

The British Library is set up in London. Until 1973 it was part of the British Museum. Today it houses Europe's largest library collection of about 80 million items.

1753

The Library of Congress is founded in Washington, USA, to serve members of Congress. The collection starts with 740 books and three maps. It has now grown to more than 100 million items.

1800

Boston Library, in the USA, becomes the world's first public library – anyone can use it, free of charge. Today there are more than 13 500 public libraries in the USA.

1848

The UK's first public libraries open, in Canterbury, Winchester, Warrington, Salford, Liverpool and Manchester. Most lend books free of charge, but some ask readers to pay one penny per book. The charges are eventually dropped.

1850s

Andrew Carnegie, a rich industrialist, establishes a fund for building public libraries. Almost 3000 libraries are built across the world with Carnegie funds.

1880s

1753 to present day

The invention of printing leads to the growth of library collections. Noble familes, such as the Medicis of Italy, build private libraries. For the first time books are stacked in bookcases rather than chained to the shelves.

1400s

Pope Nicholas V establishes the Vatican Library in the Vatican City, Italy. The library is one of the first to stock books made from paper. Until this time, most books were made from vellum, parchment or papyrus.

1451

The Bodleian Library is opened at the University of Oxford, England. Today, the library holds six million books.

1602

The first library in America is founded by the Pilgrim Fathers at Henrico, Virginia.

1620

Harvard University Library opens in the USA, with a collection of 300 books. Today it holds more than 13 million books, and is the oldest research library in the USA.

1638

Redwood Library is founded at Newport, Rhode Island. It is the oldest surviving lending library in the USA.

1747

The New York Public Library is founded in the USA. Today it has about 12 million books, making it the world's largest public library.

1895

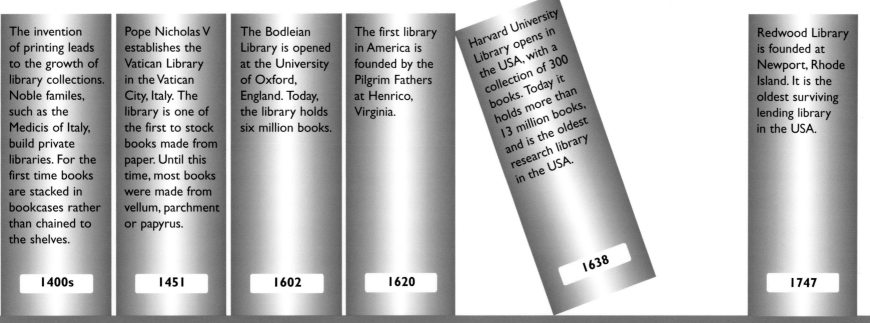

The National Library of China is set up in Beijing. The main building is the largest single library building in the world.

1909

Project Gutenberg begins. The project aims to make complete books available in electronic form. By 2001, around 10 000 texts will be accessible through the Internet.

1971

The National Library of Australia becomes the first national library to set up its own website on the Internet.

1994

The new British Library building is officially opened at St Pancras, London. It took two years to transfer the collection from the old library at the British Museum.

1998

Famous libraries

Information has been collected and preserved in libraries for more than 2500 years. The ruins of a few ancient libraries can still be seen today, although their contents disappeared long ago. Copies of a few parchments, scrolls and books still exist to tell us what they once housed. In more recent times, national libraries have built up collections running into millions of items.

⬇ The Library of Celsus was a two-storey building. The main reading area occupied one whole floor, with books stored in bays around the room. Large windows allowed light deep into the building.

The Library of Celsus, Ephesus, Turkey

Construction of the Library of Celsus, in the Roman city of Ephesus, began in 110 AD. Its builder, Gaius Julius Aquila, planned it as a memorial to his father, who is buried in a tomb under the ground floor. The building was completed 25 years later. At one time there were around 12 000 items in the library, making it one of the largest collections in the ancient world. Visitors consulted scrolls and parchments in the main reading room of the building. The library was burned down in the third century AD, leaving the shell that is still standing today.

The British Library, London

The British Library is one of the world's great libraries. At least one copy of every book published in the UK is stored there. From 1753 until the late 1990s it shared a site in London with the British Museum. By the 1970s, the library's shelves and storerooms had begun to overflow – so a new building was planned in St Pancras, north London. After 15 years of building work, the new library was officially opened to the public in 1998.

⚫ The British Library's new building at St Pancras, London, is Europe's largest national library, housing about 18 million books.

The National Library of France, Paris

In the Middle Ages, the kings of France collected manuscripts which became the basis of the Royal Library. Since 1537, one copy of every book printed in France has been added to the library. Today, the collection is known as the National Library of France, which occupies two sites in Paris. A complex of old buildings in the city centre holds millions of items on over 100 kilometres of shelving. In the suburbs, at Tolbiac, a new library has been built with more than 395 kilometres of shelving.

The Library of Congress, Washington DC, USA

The first books in this collection arrived from London in 1801. They were stored in the US Capitol, the library's first home. Today, the library occupies three massive buildings in Washington DC, housing over 100 million items in more than 450 languages. It receives a free copy of every book published in the USA. About 5000 people work at the Library of Congress. More than two million researchers and tourists visit it each year, while millions more use its services.

⚫ The reading room of the Library of Congress, in Washington DC. The library is home to 15 million books, 39 million manuscripts, 13 million photographs, 3.5 million pieces of music, and over half a million films.

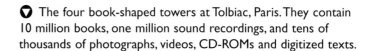

⚫ The four book-shaped towers at Tolbiac, Paris. They contain 10 million books, one million sound recordings, and tens of thousands of photographs, videos, CD-ROMs and digitized texts.

Glossary

audio book A novel or story book that has been recorded on to cassette tape. Audio books are also known as talking books.

audiovisual Involving both sight and hearing.

barcode A series of vertical lines which can be read by a computer to identify a particular item, such as a book.

bindery The department where books, magazines and newspapers are given new or replacement hardback covers.

book block The pages of a book before it is given a cover.

bookbinder A person who puts covers on books.

books on wheels A service which takes books to people who cannot travel to the library. It is usually run by volunteers.

Braille A system of printing for visually-impaired people. It uses raised dots which are read by touch.

brailler A machine like a typewriter which is used to make braille dots.

catalogue A list of items in the library's collection, including books, CDs, tapes, maps and photographs.

CD-ROM Short for compact disc read-only memory – an interactive compact disc used on a computer. The disc stores text, images and sound.

census An official count of a country's population, including information such as age, sex and occupation.

clay tablet A piece of clay used for writing on in ancient times, especially in Middle Eastern countries.

closed-circuit television reader A machine for visually-impaired people which uses a video camera to film the pages of a book. The pages are shown enlarged on a television screen.

compact disc (CD) A plastic and metal disc on which music or information is stored digitally.

conservation Looking after something carefully, such as a rare book.

cuneiform An ancient wedge-shaped form of writing used in countries in the Middle East.

desensitizer A machine at the issue desk which demagnetizes the trigger strip in a book.

Dewey Decimal System of Classification A system of numbers used to sort non-fiction books into groups, used in many libraries since 1876.

dictionary A book which lists words and their meanings in alphabetical order.

digital versatile disc (DVD) A type of CD-ROM which holds more information, especially video clips.

directory A book that lists the names of companies or people in alphabetical order, with details of their addresses and telephone numbers.

download To transfer information from one computer to another.

e-mail Electronic messages which are sent from one computer to another.

encyclopaedia A book or set of books containing information about many subjects.

endpapers The pages at the front and back of a hardback book which attach the book block to its cover.

gauze Transparent woven cloth that is used to strengthen the spines of some hardback books.

gelatine A clear substance made from meat and animal bones. It dissolves in water and sets into a jelly.

genealogy The study of family history.

glyphs Signs used in some types of ancient writing.

gold leaf A thin sheet of gold, used for stamping the title and author name on to valuable hardback books.

guillotine A sharp metal blade for trimming the edges of book blocks.

hardback A book with a hard cover.

incunable A book printed before 1500. The name comes from the Latin word *incunabula*, which means a cradle. The 1400s were known as the cradle of printing, because printing had just been invented.

Internet A worldwide network of computers linked together by telephone lines.

Japanese tissue Very thin but strong transparent paper, used to repair torn pages in books.

Kurzweil reader A machine for visually-impaired people that reads out loud the words in a book. The user listens on headphones to avoid disturbing other people in the library.

light pen A pen connected to a computer which reads a barcode.

listening booth The place where a library user listens to an audio tape or CD without disturbing other people.

local studies library The library's collection of items about the local area. It is also known as the record office.

microfiche A flat sheet of transparent plastic. It contains small photographs of the pages of a book, magazine or newspaper.

microfiche reader A machine which projects microfiche images on to a large screen.

microfilm A roll of film with pages from a book, magazine or newspaper photographed on to it at reduced size.

microfilm reader A machine which projects microfilm images on to a large screen.

mobile library A vehicle containing books, CDs, tapes and videos which travels to places some distance from the main library. Large libraries have a fleet of several vehicles.

multimedia Giving information in many forms (media), such as text, graphics, animation, video and sound.

papyrus A type of paper made from the stems of water reeds. Papyrus was used by the ancient Greeks, Egyptians and Romans.

parchment An animal skin made into a material to write on in ancient times.

parish An area that has its own church and priest.

parish register A book that lists every birth, baptism, marriage and death at a church.

reference book A book, such as an encyclopaedia or an atlas, which has to be used inside the library. It cannot be borrowed.

scroll A roll of paper or parchment used to write on.

spine The back of a book, which is strengthened with glue, thread or gauze.

teletext Information, such as news or weather reports, which is broadcast by a television channel and picked up on television sets.

tie-in A book connected to a film or a television programme.

trigger strip A metallic ribbon inside every book. Unless it is demagnetized by a librarian, it triggers an alarm at the exit.

vellum A fine parchment.

video conferencing When several people in different places have a meeting by videophone.

videophone A video camera linked to a computer. It allows two or more people who may be thousands of kilometres apart to talk and see each other at the same time.

volume Another name for a book. Encyclopaedias are often made up of several volumes.

website A set of pages on the World Wide Web with information about a particular subject.

wood pulp Wood that has been ground up and mixed with a liquid chemical. The pulp is bleached white and used to make paper.

World Wide Web A vast collection of information available on the Internet.

Index

First published in Great Britain in 2000 by
Belitha Press Limited
London House, Great Eastern Wharf
Parkgate Road, London SW11 4NQ

Copyright © Belitha Press Limited 2000
Text copyright © John Malam 2000

Library cutaway illustrations: David Cuzik
All other illustrations: William Donohoe
Series editor: Mary-Jane Wilkins
Editor: Russell Mclean
Designer: Guy Callaby
Picture researcher: Diana Morris
Consultant: Ayyub Malik
Series concept: Christine Hatt

If you would like to comment on this book,
e-mail the author at johnmalam@aol.com

The author and publishers wish to thank
the John Rylands University Library of
Manchester, Manchester Central Library,
and Cheshire County Council (Libraries
and Archives) for helping with this book.

ISBN 1 84138 054 7

Printed in China

British Library Cataloguing in Publication Data
for this book is available from the British Library.

Picture acknowledgements: Richard Bryant/Arcaid:
29cl. Paul Raferty/Arcaid: 29br. Nigel Sitwell/
Hutchison Library: 28b. Earl Young/Trip: 29tr.